The Surface of the Lit World

The Hollis Summers Poetry Prize

GENERAL EDITOR: DAVID SANDERS

Named after the distinguished poet who taught for many years at Ohio University and made Athens, Ohio, the subject of many of his poems, this competition invites writers to submit unpublished collections of original poems. The competition is open to poets who have not published a book-length collection as well as to those who have.

Full and updated information is available on the Hollis Summers Poetry Prize web page: ohioswallow.com/poetry_prize

Meredith Carson, *Infinite Morning*

Memye Curtis Tucker, *The Watchers*

V. Penelope Pelizzon, *Nostos*

Kwame Dawes, *Midland*

Allison Eir Jenks, *The Palace of Bones*

Robert B. Shaw, *Solving for X*

Dan Lechay, *The Quarry*

Joshua Mehigan, *The Optimist*

Jennifer Rose, *Hometown for an Hour*

Ann Hudson, *The Armillary Sphere*

Roger Sedarat, *Dear Regime: Letters to the Islamic Republic*

Jason Gray, *Photographing Eden*

Will Wells, *Unsettled Accounts*

Stephen Kampa, *Cracks in the Invisible*

Nick Norwood, *Gravel and Hawk*

Charles Hood, *South × South: Poems from Antarctica*

Alison Powell, *On the Desire to Levitate*

Shane Seely, *The Surface of the Lit World*

The Surface of the Lit World

Poems

Shane Seely

OHIO UNIVERSITY PRESS

ATHENS

Ohio University Press, Athens, Ohio 45701

ohioswallow.com

To obtain permission to quote, reprint, or otherwise reproduce or distribute material
from Ohio University Press publications, please contact our rights and permissions
department at (740) 593-1154 or (740) 593-4536 (fax).

Printed in the United States of America
Ohio University Press books are printed on acid-free paper ⊛ ™

25 24 23 22 21 20 19 18 17 16 15   5 4 3 2 1

Library of Congress Cataloging-in-Publication Data
Seely, Shane.
 [Poems. Selections]
 Surface of the lit world : poems / Shane Seely.
     pages cm. — (Hollis Summers poetry prize)
 Summary: "In The Surface of the Lit World, Shane Seely draws on a wide range of
sources — from personal memory to biblical narrative — to explore the stories that
we tell ourselves about ourselves, the ways in which we make meaning of our lives.
Seely delves into the ways in which family and environment shape us. Poems ranging
from terse, meditative lyrics to more direct narratives examine the relationship
between what lies visible on the lit surface and what lies just beneath. In addition
to first-person autobiographical narratives, there are ekphrastic poems; poems that
explore narratives from mythology and religion; and poems based on news reports,
radio stories, and audio recordings. Regardless of the approach, the central questions
are the same: How do we sense the world we live in? What do the institutions to
which we turn for meaning — family, religion, art, literature, science — offer us, and
in what ways do they fail us? The answers may depend on where we dare to look"—
Provided by publisher.
 ISBN 978-0-8214-2148-2 (paperback) — ISBN 978-0-8214-4512-9 (pdf)
 I. Title.
 PS3619.E356A6 2015
 811'.6—dc23
                                2015001222

Acknowledgments

Thanks to the editors of the following journals, who were generous enough to publish poems from this collection, occasionally in slightly different forms.

Antioch Review: Preschool Race, Seen through a Bus Window
Architrave Press: Anthology
Birmingham Poetry Review: Forest Cemetery
Cave Wall: Chain Saw at Dusk
Confrontation: Isaac's Lament
Cumberland River Review: Centralia; Lost Ring
Exit 7: Stick; Sucker Fish
Florida Review: Noon Bus in a Heat Wave; The Orangutans of the Omaha Zoo
Hayden's Ferry Review: Danaë
Measure: Sonnet for the Pennsylvania Mountain Lion
New Madrid: The Opossum
Passages North: Rehearsal for an Execution; For the Swamp King of Kalispell
Poet Lore: The Frozen Pond
Seneca Review: Walt Whitman at the Irish Festival, Syracuse, New York: Four Snapshots
Southern Poetry Review: Still Life with Mice
The Southern Review: Partial Solar Eclipse; You Fell Forward on Both Knees
Sweet: Spider Laisse; Laisse for an Insect on an Open Book of Poems
Tampa Review: After Stanley Kunitz
Tar River Poetry: The Fox
Valparaiso Poetry Review: View-Master

"These Fine Collapses" and "The Cinder Woman" reprinted by permission of *The Normal School*, Copyright 2013 by Shane Seely.

"Walt Whitman at the Irish Festival, Syracuse, New York: Four Snapshots" was reprinted in *Visiting Walt: Poems Inspired by the Life & Work of Walt Whitman*, edited by Sheila Coghill and Thom Tammaro (University of Iowa Press, 2003).

Gratitude is due as well to the early readers of these poems, without whom they would not have found their forms: Katy Didden, Jeff Hamilton, Lisa Pepper, Stephanie Schlaifer, Jason Sommer, and Chuck Sweetman. Thanks to my colleagues at UMSL for their collegiality and support. And thanks, always, to Sonia, for every page.

for Sonia —

like a circle

in the sun

We had, it seems, loved the planet and loved our lives, but could no longer remember the way of them. We got the light wrong.

—Annie Dillard, "Total Eclipse"

Contents

I

Descent

Always after dark, the night before the trashman came,
I lifted each black sack bulging from its metal can

and piled it outside. Even with my back turned, I could see
my parents in the warm light of the kitchen window,

their conversation pantomimed. Above the garage door,
a mercury lamp spilled a pool of bluish light not far
    enough

to illuminate the whole driveway, which curved in its
    descent
around a brushy bank. By the time I'd hauled my burden

halfway down the drive, the only light was stars. The
    mailbox
had a ghoulish face, and every tree had hands. Behind

the boxwood, something coughed and snarled. A ghost
sighed into the wind and kicked a stone that clattered
    out ahead,

as if in warning of the dangers waiting where the driveway
met the road. And so I raised my lone defense,

the lone defense of children sunk in darkness everywhere:
I sang. Not well or even sure of what I sang, I murmured
    first

then called more clearly against all lurking terrors—I
    pitched
my boy's falsetto against the black glass of rising night,

as if to crack it, as if to punch a gap that light might run
    through.
I sang the bags to their resting place, then turned to face

the path, the silent trees, the surface of the lit world. I sang
returning, too, wary of the fate of those who look behind.

The Fledged Boy

The versions of the story you have heard
aren't true: these are my father's wings
in the same way that this is his nose.
Not by him, but of him. I was born
with an egg tooth and a pale fringe
of feathers down each arm. Like he
was. He taught me how to hide them
beneath the loose clothes my mother sewed,
sleeves wider than a marmot's burrow,
but he taught me too to groom them,
to keep this coastal dust out of their grain.
Each night I'd pull my left arm then
my right across my chest and smooth
each plume between my fingers
till it shone. This is how I knew
that I belonged to him.

                     How could I
refuse, then, when he said that we
would fly out of that tower home.
I'd never used my wings before, not
even to soften a fall when I jumped
from a tall rock by the shore. I wanted
no one to see me, wanted no one
to know what we knew. When I
removed my shirt, the sun glowed
like a candled egg in the single window
of our cell. I felt my feathers stand
in the air that leaked in off the water.

My father looked at them, and I
could see that he was proud.
He asked if I knew what I needed
to do. I told him the truth, that I did.

Rehearsal for an Execution

at the Louisiana State Penitentiary at Angola

Twice a year he rises and goes to his death
in the farthest room of the state penitentiary
rises from the warm breath of his wife still
sleeping and into the dark of the morning
looks in on his children sleeping and still and leaves
    them
before even the birds have shuddered awake
before the grass blades lift before
the magnolia blossoms open their delicate throats
to the morning—

He leaves them in darkness
his headlights slash it and it seals around him absorbs
the little metal vessel carrying him
into the night's fathomless body
at the prison they're waiting the warden
the officers with their cruel mouths and trustless
eyes the priest who will pray for his soul again
always the same prayer the same
unreconciled life each detail
is consistent the small
audience behind the glass the official huddle
around him he is bound shackled silent
down the pale green hallway
his chains clank simulating drama
the warden barks and the heavy doors

open and the green table
greets him again

Sometimes he conjures a criminal history
like something seen on television
in the middle of a sleepless night
bodies sunk in swamps across four states turning
filmy eyes toward a cruel moon
or stacked like cordwood in the toolshed
until the neighbor's dog
digs a hole beneath the door
or the corpse discovered
in six plastic bags
at the bottom of a lake imagines
florid tattoos a casual skill
with a knife—
though more often he remembers
his own crimes his daughter's
hot face slapped a welter
of tears he thinks what debt
his life might ease as some men
do as they are hooded
as they rest their heads against the table
smell the leather
as it is tightened
a hand swabs his arm with alcohol
the last gesture to be rehearsed
each time he imagines
the needle's bite the cool surge
in his veins

Hooded and splayed he can hear them
those who have lain as he lies now
their breath as it suffers
and seizes as the eddy of chemicals
scorches their hearts these men vessels
offered upon a table with whom
he shares this single posture
though only he
knows what happens
when the straps are loosened
and the hood removed

View-Master

Each Christmas, as the mother read from the family Bible
of the birth of Christ by Christmas lights
that spangled the Fraser fir in the living room,

the boy turned the square eyes of the old View-Master
toward the light that spilled in from the kitchen.
He watched the story figured frame by frame

in three dust-enhanced dimensions: there,
the gravid wife upon a donkey; there, the innkeep
pointing to the stable. The angels seemed cast

in smoothest porcelain, and the wise men posed
like mannequins. And then the Christ child, son of man,
brilliant in his nest of hay: his cheek had the curve
        and color

of the plastic apples in the bowl on the dining table,
so red and round that the boy would sometimes reach
        for one
even though he knew they weren't real.

Danaë

Artemisia Gentileschi, 1612 (oil on copper)

Witness Zeus as golden coins cascading
in the dark air of Danaë's locked room,
collecting in the crevice of her naked thighs,
squeezed between her clenching fingers.
A marble roundness at belly and calf, a breath
of pink at cheek and throat, head thrown back,
eyes lidded in her pleasure's dark retreats.
The draped hair, the scarlet coverlet
beneath her on the bed.

                    And look beyond her
to the maid, clothed in rough fabrics
to the wrist—her scarved head turned upward,
turned away from her writhing mistress—
who lifts her dark blue skirts to catch the gold
that rains from nowhere.

                    Imagine the women,
their chamber as close and quiet as a closed
mouth, hearing the first soft thud of a coin
on the bed. Then another, then more, rattling
the stones of the floor, pelting the dark walls,
and they turn their faces toward the strange light
now filling the air with gold, each coin
imprinted with the visage of a god.

Partial Solar Eclipse

The air was warm, still
pregnant with light. We looked
down, knowing

how the sun might
strike the eye. Some, drawn
to the same green hillside, looked up

through welder's goggles
or studied shadows
inside pinhole boxes.

The astronomer capped a filter
on his telescope. Beneath
a nearby tree, the shadow of the moon

cut a slip from every patch of light
that fell between the leaves. We stood
in the open, laid the fingers

of one hand
across the fingers of the other
and gathered light like trees.

We scattered crescent suns
in the grass beneath our hands.

Lost Ring

My finger drawn thin in the cold sun
of late December, the ring slid
insensibly somewhere into nowhere,
invisible among the understuff
like a gnome's treasure. The first sign
was the sensation of the raw air
around the little band of skin
the ring had rested on. Had it
fallen in the leaves I'd left
unraked about the yard, now sogged
into a mat between the tufts of grass?
Had it flown off when I threw
into the weedy edge the dregs
I'd dredged from the birdbath's
almost-ice? Had it rolled among
the dead stalks of the asters left
unpruned? So much goes overgrown
if not attended to. I keep
imagining its glint against
the lowered sun, its silver O
not quite the O it was
before the world reforged it. And the line
inscribed on its inside face, gone
inscrutable beyond the threshold
of the read world. The sun
stubs itself against the trees.
Here's my hand, un-

inscribed, empty as the ring now lost
to the history of dirt, now remembered
by the small weight of its absence.

Chain Saw at Dusk

I watch as my neighbor
takes down the Chinese elm

that dropped a limb
in last spring's late ice.

Its branches shake as the saw—
too small, a saw for wrist-thick limbs—

whines and rattles into the heartwood
until the crown plunges, and the sky

opens a little more, gives
a little more of the purplish gray

it keeps in its herringbone clouds
as the light fails. Confident now,

the saw sets down to its work,
snarling through the elm's thin tips.

The surrounding trees turn
silhouette. And now

someone else is swinging an axe
into the new, wet logs, its *thuck thuck*

in the cool air a rhythm
beneath the rough keen of the saw.

The old song draws me
from my desk to the window,

which I open to the familiar smells
of sawdust and gasoline,

to the sounds of the labor
and the feel of evening air.

And what comes in, too—
no, he was already here—

is my father
and the sound of his saw

as he cut the wood
we'd burn all winter,

and the cool, fumy smell
on his clothes

when night fell
and he finally came inside.

The Opossum

The opossum played dead, grinned
grotesquely in the sodium light of the night-yard
where my father had carried it
from the dark fringe of the forest.
Moth shadows darkened
its lolling tongue, its yellow teeth,
its gray body curled
in rigor. But if you lifted it
by the thick rope of its tail,
you would feel the body's warmth
as it gripped your palm.
Lay it down again. Watch
the grand performance,
the commitment to the role,
the deep, animal concentration
a feigned death requires.
In bear country, playing dead
is last resort—the hope
that the bear will tire
of the bloody wreck of your carcass
and leave you in the brush
to feed on later. You must commit yourself
to the artful rendering of your death.
You must be so dead that you forget
that you're alive. We watched
from the window the opossum
resurrected—first the tail
unfurled, the snout lifted slightly,

and then it rose from the damp grass
and waddled toward the forest,
its coarse fur standing as though harrowed.

On the Recording of Weldon Kees Reading "Relating to Robinson"

in the muffled distance, you can hear
a woman's voice. You can't tell what she's saying,
and certainly not to whom, but there it is,
in the silences between his lines, as once,
on the telephone with a distant friend,
you might have heard your neighbor's voice
in the silences of your own speech
as your conversations crowded the copper wire.
Maybe she's the voice on a radio playing softly
in an uncurtained second-story room.
Maybe she's a palimpsest, a lost
reader of a lost poem about lovers
coming to in morning, her voice not quite
erased by Kees' noir deadpan, by the could-be
Robinson's harrowed oracle. She sounds
like a ghost, her mumble arising
from the static—as if to say
I'm here, I'm here, I'm still still here.

These Fine Collapses

And yet these fine collapses are not lies
—Hart Crane, "Chaplinesque"

The poet at the microphone said *Hart Crane*
and the man at the front table, drunk,
threw himself against his chair

and shouted, *What the fuck*
do you know about Hart Crane?
As though this were Crane himself,

back from the deep, wet on the deck
of the steamship, back now
and angry, furious at being

the subject of the sort of idle
patter spoken at poetry readings.
And the speaker paused, perhaps

wondering what wound he had struck
in this man at the mention
of Crane's name, what spiked pit

he'd fallen into, what old anger
rose up now before him, spat
Bullshit, and staggered to the door.

It was cold outside, and dark
in the alleys, dark enough to be
depthless, the lights all shrunken

in the face of the evening. We watched
as the man passed the windows,
which were glazed with the steam of our breath.

The Cinder Woman

I believe you burned
from the inside
out—the pool of ash

you left, the scorched TV,
the shoes your feet
still filled not even

black with smoke—
and I believe your body
was the sun,

that it blazed up
from the chair
in that dim living

room, that the empty
air was filled
with light.

As you sat, a pillar,
a finger of fire,
altar and offering,

were voices
singing? Or was there
only smoke?

Oh Cinder Woman, not
your blackened bone, not
the soot stain on the ceiling

where you died: I
love you. I, who am
damp tinder.

I, who am
flameless as the sea.

Isaac's Lament

He took the wood from me and bound my wrists
and ankles like a ram's. I did not fight,
but lay there, waiting as he struck the flint
and breathed the ember into flame. He kissed
my face and said my name one time, as slight
winds lifted dust into his eyes, then turned
and drew the knife. I watched the oiled blade glint
against the sun, and I—who would have burned

himself alive to please this man—I smiled.
Knife poised, he touched my hair and said
he loved me more than any father loved a son.
I showed his knife my throat; his eyes grew wild
with awful love. My reprieve came then, un-
binding me from him. I lived instead.

Sucker Fish

Most we just threw back, but this one
was so large—18 inches anyway—
and larger yet

my child pride at catching it—
my father pulled the hook
and slipped the sucker in the pouch

of his fishing vest. At home,
a picture first: me smiling,
still wading in my rubber boots,

the dead eye of the fish, its scales
the color of tarnished coins, its length
measured in a child's hands.

And then my father cleaned it—
removed the entrails, the head, the scaly
skin—and set it in a pan to fry.

Beside it on the plate, sliced
dry bread to pull down any bones
that might get caught.

A sucker's flesh is full of bones.
Greedy in my pride,
I swallowed hard.

Early Postcard from Paradise

With a shovel blade, my father killed the snake
that rattled the grass my new and only world was.
I was young enough to be forgiven for
my unsteady pace, my emotive grunts,
my tendency to fall. The snake was something
to protect me from—it seemed to make
the very grass hiss. My father didn't know
from what bright recess it had crawled or why,
but the blade bit six inches deep into the sod
beneath its belly scales, which were checkered
black and creamy white when the snake's two halves
curled in a spasm of surprise like any dead thing.
Only then, when the snake lay segmented
on the shovel, could my father see
that this had been no rattler, but a simple
milk snake, drawn from the shed where it
had lived on mice by the same sun that drew
us out—the sun that warmed the shovel blade
and the shrunk ribbon of the snake, that lit
the little murder scene, saying: now you know.

II

After Stanley Kunitz

It was an only
child's game: the spongy
egg of the football,
worn already in
the spots on which
my fingers gripped it,
thrown into the air,
chased across the grass
and caught with a leap
or a dive, or, as I
stumbled heroically,
plucked from my sneakers'
grass-stained laces.
I knew just how high
and far I could throw it
and still chase it down,
knew how to run
with my chin in the air,
tracking the wobbling
ball, how to ease up
then burst forward
to heighten the drama.
A catch, a spin, I stumble
and fall. Second down.
This time, the ball
is pitched wide, a sprint
to the sideline, and, as I
leap into the pine's shadow

the end zone is, I call
the name of the player
I'm pretending. I, my own
hero, my own calling
crowd, my own opponent
reaching to pull me down.

You Fell Forward on Both Knees

not in genuflection, no, not
some unexpected return
to your inherited Catholicism:
you fell, pitched from the lip of an uneven
sidewalk, and skidded on all fours,
your head hanging. You looked
for a moment like a woman in pursuit
of a fallen button, which must be
a kind of prayer itself: a belief
that a lost thing might be recovered, might
signal to the one who seeks it
by casting back a little light
from a shadowed corner.
But whatever god's name
you grunted in the sidewalk's ear
was not an invocation
but a curse, and if we prayed,
it was the hard prayer of attention
to the ugly world: your bloody
shins, the mosaics of grit
below your kneecaps,
the mockingbird
that went on singing. You sat
atop a low retaining wall and offered
me your knees, and I knelt,
and, taking each calf
in turn into my hands,
whispered cures to your open wounds.

Noon Bus in a Heat Wave

His son
wears the same
thick glasses
he wears

and calls
upon his father
to name
each car

that passes
the wide windows:
Dad, what's that
one, that

one, that one.
Leaving the
boy with his
mother, the man

works his way
to the front
of the bus, one seat
at a time.

In his left hand
is a styrofoam cup,
lid pierced
by a mangled straw,

and in his right
an instant
lottery scratch-off
ticket, which

he gouges
with the nail
of his right thumb,
such that

his hand twists
into a sort of claw
as he leans tight
over the ticket

each time he sits,
each station
of his progress
to the front of the bus.

He looks
the other riders
in their faces,
and they look

away, let their
gazes drift
to the high apartments
bordering the park,

to the thin
brown-skinned

swimmers
returning from the pool.

Dad, the boy
says, *that car
looks weird.*
Dad, look.

The man looks back, and
then ahead. The lottery
ticket softens
in his damp hand.

For the Swamp King of Kalispell

When they found your ragged carcass by the stream,
torn by bears and ravens till the rib cage
glistened, even the skull picked clean—just the hide left,
flung like a fatty coat across the shoulders—we felt
all the predictable emotions: sadness
at your majesty cut down, revulsion at death's
indignity, wonder—a few said, and the rest
agreed—that you had lived at all, a beast
so broad of back and thick of tine, you seemed
of an age before these valleys
grew heavy with our homes. In your honor, hunters shot
a round into the dirt. The women cried
in the center of the town. Remember the Swamp King,
the mayor said, and we all swore we would.

That first night, though, men had killed their headlights
and idled to a stop above the stream,
thumbing their bone saws,
hoping the field mice had left your antlers.
At least one little boy mimed shooting you,
made a rifle noise while sighting down his index finger.
And each of us, in some dark hollow of his heart,
was relieved to see you lying there, all tattered skin
and mouse-gnawed bone, lying there
in a form that we could master.

Sonnet for the Pennsylvania Mountain Lion

Ray claims he saw you with his own two eyes,
then tells me of the trappers' stories, how
you tore a raccoon from its trap, then tried—
on that same night—to take down Yoder's cow.

You are one of Ray's many lies. It's clear:
the deer that nibble apples on the hill,
that pause at night along the road, don't fear
you, don't startle at your scent. But still,

I'm quick to see you in the half-lit dark
spirit past the springhouse, a flake of moon
falling from your eye. I'm quick to mark
your track where sun has baked spring's mud all June.

Ray says he'll kill you true and take your head
to mount; I'd rather see you false than dead.

Dürer's Rhinoceros

Albrecht Dürer, 1515 (woodcut)

Its armor, hammered and burnished
by no one but God—

its wedge head plate-scaled,
its horn upturning and spear sharp—

Dürer turns his graver to the woodblock,
presses into the soft grain

the heavy beast, its whiskered jaw,
the whorled scales of its shoulder plate,

the horn with which, wrote Pliny,
it might gore its rival, the elephant—

it must have measured the crowds
in the port by that horn,

as the spice traders' awe
rippled back through the city—

the children come running
and gawking, daring

someone to poke its belly
with a stick—

On Dürer's block, the heavy
triangular head

dips toward barren ground,
at horn and tail the frame encroaches—

the close quarters of the trading ship,
the wracked timbers groaning

at the southern edge
of the dark continent,

the strange beast mute
above its portion of rice—

What sounds it must have made
from those heavy lips!

How frightening the creature
that frowns fearless

in the stunned world!

Laisse for an Insect on an Open Book of Poems

Little glyph, small enough to crawl inside
the O you've landed near—oh, what am I
to you? I must be landscape, weather, sky:
mere circumstance. I'd like to think my size
makes me invisible to you.
                              Just now,
I nearly smudged you with my thumb, made powder
of your lacy wings and thread-legs, ground
you into the grain of the paper.
                                    About
my reasons, I'll say nothing, whether by
accident or grace you haven't died.
I am no more deft than I am kind.
Still, on the page, beneath this noonish light,

you just might be a consonant or vowel
blown from an ancient alphabet and out
a dusty window, a runic mark without
translation in a tongue I can't pronounce.

Teaching English at the Chrysler Plant

One, asked to name his favorite poet
from the course, chose Marianne Moore
because she wrote "Poetry,"
which begins, "I, too, dislike it."
And I smiled, understanding
that we had an understanding: they
endured my part-time effort, and I
endured their light resentment
of the burden this reading was:
they hated Williams'
Tom in *The Glass Menagerie*
for his self-pity, all the more
when I told them Tom was Williams'
stand-in, and that his apology to Laura
was Williams' own apology
to his own troubled sister.
Some worked shifts after class
and some before, and all
were tired, tired — they'd all gone
to the lake that weekend, couldn't we
talk about that, hadn't any poets
ever gone to the lake
in any of their poems? Wordsworth
wasn't what they had in mind, so I
brought Levine in, read to them from
What Work Is so that they might
see themselves in literature, sepia-toned
and burnished before their loud machines,

until someone interrupted to ask if I had
any poems about love—*not*
regular relationships, you know,
real love. In a few years, the plant
would close, and Chrysler would turn over
like a toad. I doubt that any of them
turned to poems for their news then,
whatever news they'd find there. They
thought about the lake, the summer weekend's
long, unbroken line, the promise
they read across the surface of the water—
opaque, glass-smooth, dazzled with light.

Walt Whitman at the Irish Festival, Syracuse, New York: Four Snapshots

I

He hugs each policeman in turn,
and they laugh and turn a deep American red
beneath their blue caps.

II

He dances a jig with an old man
and a young girl
and a man inexplicably dressed
in a horned Viking helmet
and Scottish tartan kilt.
Sweat beads on his forehead
and his white beard tosses like a wave.
He dances badly, and long
into the night.

III

A man hawks buttons saying,
"Kiss me, I'm Irish."
He kisses him.

IV

He jumps the stage
(we did not know he played the mandolin)
to sing a song. It is a song no one
has heard before, and yet the band
remembers how to play it.
Everyone knows the words,
and everyone dances.

Stick

The dog has a stick that angles awkward from his mouth
and the pup, standing parallel and reaching, wants it.
     The dog

moves in a circle precisely slow enough to keep the stick
beyond the pup's reach barely. The pup turns in her
     own arc,

larger than his by the width of his body, the smaller of two
planets orbiting the same sun, desire. Then she gets hold

of the stick's free end, sets her feet, and twists. The stick
cracks, splits. The circling stops. Wanting a kind of
     fairness

there, I hope they'll settle in, each with half the stick, to
some meditative chewing. But the pup drops her half

and returns jealous to his shoulder, to their spooling
spin across the yard. The stick's no prize. The wanting is.

Orpheus Charming the Animals

Gustave Surand, c. 1880 (oil on canvas)

Surand's Orpheus, drunk with song,
barefoot in the mountains, wearing
only the gauziest loincloth — the bird-flocked
mountain pool reflecting sky, the lyre,
throat-delicate, resounding — feels the prick
of sweat along his scalp as the first tiger
rustles from the underbrush
and sniffs his naked foot. And then
a second tiger and a group of lions
out of nowhere, crowding in. When a leopard
turns belly up like a tabby in the path, he
sees the claws, the body bending
on its iron springs. He sees himself
inverted in the big cats' eyes —
tender neck, warm blood pulsing
at belly and groin. He had thought nothing
of the birds as they assembled, even
the flamingoes now bowing on their stick legs
in the shallows. He had sung to birds before.
Like to like, he thought, and tuned his lyre.
The big cats, though: their expectant faces,
the menace in their calm. He sings and sings.

The Kite Flyers of Forest Park

There are the serious ones,
out only on the windiest days,

their box kites climbing the air
until they look like scraps of bright paper

rattling the thermals. The serious ones
tie their kites to their folding chairs

and leave them higher than hawks,
more tethered for holding so high.

The ones we love to watch,
though, fly the cheap plastic kites—

brittle rib, cellophane wing.
They judder and dance overhead,

they drop like shot pheasants,
they struggle to gather the breeze. Once,

we watched a young father toss his kite in the air
and sprint into the wind. The kite

wobbled then rose, dipped
and then climbed. When the kid squealed,

his dad turned and returned—and the breeze
climbed the kite's back and the kite

dragged in the grass as he ran. These
are the ones that we watch:

still grasping the magic of wind,
still startled to look up

at the cloud-painted sky
and see an almost-bird struggling to fly.

Preschool Race, Seen through a Bus Window

Across the street from the Catholic church, five runners
on the empty soccer field:

two boys in white tee shirts neck
and neck

two boys in polos close behind
and one boy

the last boy—
as the sun blooms above the church spire

brightening the field's green—
skipping

III

Silm: Four Definitions from the Estonian

Eye

The window frames the scene: the day's last bees
drugged at the mint's tassels, the daylilies
defeated by heat, the rose gone brown.
In the birdbath, nothing
but an early acorn's cracked husk—
the squirrel's litter—
and the brown dregs
of evaporated rain. And then
a goldfinch lights among the coneflowers.

Bud

Sharpened by drought, the coneflowers
lean into the chain-link. Beyond, anemones
bulge as though holding their breath. This
is how I planned it: the garden
a cascade of bloom until the killing
frost, as though the world returned a color
for each it took away.

Stitch

The goldfinch blazes
in a diamond of chain-link
before he darts to the coneflower's seedhead
to pluck the brown spines.
He rides the stalk as it tilts
beneath his weight, scattering
the husks with his beak
into the weedy margin.
He darts to the fence, to the flower,
to the fence, to the flower,
drawing tight the heat-thick air.

Floodgate

This evening, even through the heat,
we taste fall in the air, as the people in the valley
must taste each spring in their river
the first of the mountains' melted snow.

Gathering Wood before Rain

The chain saw speaks
against the dead tree

in a voice loud
and querulous.

The rain's in the air,
it will come, sure

as when it comes
it will fall.

See the oak's
brown leaves turn

over, the red shingles
of the maples

shiver. Bring the
dead snag down

and piece it
into carrying

lengths—the rain's
coming, and after

rain, snow.

A Low Wall

From the wet clay
of the inchoate
spring, from among
the damp whips
of dandelion roots,
from among the
sandstone crumbling
back into sand, any
secrets accreted
revealed only
to the first bulbs
of the crocus and
snowdrop, I,
loosening the
heavy soil where
I will lay in
a low wall, a
narrative of order,
pull up on the tines
of my fork a slow
knot of three snakes,
each no longer
than my hand and
dead-cold, barely
moving, still sealed
in their winter—
what can you do,
having uncovered

three snakes buried
like a charm
for the season
but return them,
forget them, layer
back on the clay,
the thick, weedy
sod, and call for
the blind blazing
eye of the sun
to lift its low arc
through the bud-
swollen trees—
what can you do
but bury the
snakes and wait
for the sun,
for the old ritual
of temporary
resurrection.

Bat in the House

The skin-wing thrum
only maybe heard.

The skein of its traverse
tightening the rooms,

drawing us up
from sleep. The little

woody creak
of its voice. We turn

the lights on and
it panics for a darker

corner. The whole house
awake now in its fear or

(the dogs) its predatory
curiosity. I am unsure

what kind of man
I am. I kill

the lights, slide
the windows open.

Give the night
back to the night.

The Late Deluge

On Two Paintings by J. M. W. Turner
(1843, oil on canvas)

I. Shade and Darkness: The Evening of the Deluge

> *The moon put forth her sign of woe, unheeded.*

The sun's blurred aperture recedes
or is eaten by the swirl of evening
darkness not the swirl of any
evening—someone walking home
or looking from a window up would say
be ready for a storm. But the figures
in the yellow bower, lazing
in their afterglow, do not look up.
What they know of storms
has tossed them here together, shadowed
in the failing light: her head
upon his naked shoulder, his arm
across her naked hip.
                    Beyond,
the animals in pairs begin to congregate:
against the plume of rising dark,
field beasts wait with tigers, deer,
a baboon resting on its knuckles
also waits, its mate obscured
in the spreading tarry blackness.
The lovers sleep. A shock of black
weighs down the sky. Something
scored like runes descends
into the last blue tatters—birds
arriving two by two.

II. Light and Colour: The Morning after the Deluge—Moses Writing the Book of Genesis

Hope's harbinger, ephemeral as the summer fly . . .

The sun returns blood-rimmed, a clotted yolk,
so bright that Moses disappears almost
inside it—the brazen serpent stabbed
into the mountaintop, Moses seated
as though in air.
               Below,
the faces of the damned
float in water scorched yellow
by the sun. Where are our lovers,
caught sleeping, as lovers must
always be, in their yellow bower?
Did they wake to water rising
on their skin, measuring itself
against and then beyond them as
it rose? Did they let themselves be
taken as love had taken them, let
themselves be lifted, turned inside
the current as the dark branch
of night fell hard? What else
could they do? They reached
to find again each other's bodies,
felt the water leaching out the heat.
Above them, hidden in the dark,
thick clouds poured out
their angry rain. Now, a swirl
of faces in the ebbing flood,
their open mouths dark stones.
The fetid water shrinks to pools, revealing
all that has been broken and been lost.

Spider Laisse

Unknotting knots of blankets tied in sleep
the night before, I find a tiny creature:
a spider shaken from its dark now seeks
another dark, now spiders across the sheet
toward whatever safe spot might relieve
it of its sudden pain of light and fear.
In the bathroom, where you're brushing your teeth,
you don't hear my startled gasp at seeing
it. I lay my hand, palm up, between
the spider and your pillow's shadowed pleats.
It raises filamentous legs to feel
along my edge. No recluse, wolf, or weaver,
this spider is a stranger, strange to me
as my hand is to him: its warmth, its creases,
its sudden pose of slack passivity.
The spider skirts my hand and disappears
over the bed's far edge, leaving only
a strand of thread marking his retreat.
Could I blame him? What platform could appear
that I would not suspect was mere deceit?
In what great reaching hand would I believe?

Anthology

I pressed the jack-in-the-pulpit
between the pages
of the unabridged dictionary
along with snapdragon,
mayapple, buttercup—
coltsfoot flattened in the C's,
forget-me-nots pressed
between *remember*
and *remorse*, the trillium
between *dearth* and *death*.
The fat stalk of the jack
cracked the book's spine, refused
to press the way the others
pressed and then emerged:
tamed, artificed, opened flat
for any dilettante to stick
his nose in. The jack
stained the book with purple
juice six pages deep
on either side. Saying, *this*
is how I am pronounced.
This is what I mean.

Still Life with Mice

Lodewik Susi, 1619 (oil on panel)

The split face of the foremost apple,
its seeds, varnished husks of arsenic,
laid bare inside their chambers, browns
before your eyes. Beyond, the walnut
rests cracked open like a brain
presented in its pan. The citrus fruits
are knobbed and lumped: inside,
the hidden pith, the desiccating jewels.
This is the surgeon's table, the body
on display, the pink moment
lost already. The temptation
of the ornate handle of the knife:
to cut again. Halve the companion
apple, already spotted brown.
The only things here that don't know
death are the mice that skulk
among the fruit, already gnawing
at the unshelled almond—
they've cracked the shell of another
one nearby—and you, of course.

The Frozen Pond

How odd it looks, this man slumped, drunk,
at the pickup's wheel in a flat pan of white—
the pines a green fringe, the painter's merest
gesture of landscape. The road had swirled
to white, the snow so light in the cold spangle
of January, so soft-seeming, and the truck
such a muscular extension of the man, so over-
confident. And so the man spun himself
into this silent field so white he must
shield his eyes against it—it says nothing,
that white, nothing. And the first bass crack
of the ice below says nothing, too, in any
human language, but the second comes
with a jolt to the truck like a missed step,
like a foot falling in a shallow hole, and
the man sits up and grabs the steering wheel.
The horn bleats into the trees. The whole world
constricts to the image of sunlight on a shard
of ice. Everything falls into suspension:
the man, the truck, the ice crystals riding the air,
the sound of the horn in the trees, the words
the man would speak if he had words to speak—
all of it, trapped between the cold, empty air
and the dark water still below.

The Stone Garden

Poseidon's just another god
taking what he wants,
and what he wants is her—
renowned across the sun-wracked rocks of Greece
for her sword-shivering
loveliness, her dark cascade
of hair, her virgin body deep
in robes, Athena's
maid: Medusa. He comes on
like a tidal wave, leaves
a shipwreck of a girl—
driftwood legs, stinging jellies in her eyes, hair
a tangle of kelp. Athena
breathes her curse. Medusa
screams as her skin
begins to scale.

+ + +

That hair
that men had rowed the swelled Aegean
to tangle in their hands, that honey
spun to thread, rises up
a nest of vipers now. The eyes
shrunk back, the skin
livid like a drowned girl's
skin. Against the dank
cave rock, the incessant

hissing of the snakes.
Track back to the Parthenon
a trail of living stone:
chert birds sagging branches,
a marble doe and fawn, the tinker
burned to granite on the road. As each
body stiffened—bones of quartz,
the gut a pouch of river stones
before the skin sets—what
must the girl have thought?
In each face she searched,
she saw a stricken terror
she remembered as her own.

+ + +

The men
still come. They're driven now
by a different lust: to test themselves
against her ugliness—the woman
grown powerful, grotesque. Outside
the cave, the woods are filled
with statuary, a garden
of murdered would-be murderers,
each a souvenir: his widened
eyes, extended blade. His mouth
gone frozen slack. His breath the sound
of wind across the cave.

The Weedy Thicket

The rabbit, dead, clamped at the nape
in the cat's jaws, nearly drags, it is so long,
on the concrete as the cat runs
from its hunting ground to some hidden spot

to feed. The rabbit was one that hunkered
mornings near the oxeyes in the yard, watchful
as a rabbit cannot not be and be alive—

was one that crept into the garden
to trim the rough fringe from the lettuces, was one
that darted, if the dogs spotted it, frozen
in its camouflage, through the too-small hole

in the chain-link that it could find and enter
at full speed, then off among the weedy thicket
down the block. Why does some part of me,

some unhappy part, insist that we should get
what we deserve? The cat was turned out
by the neighbor woman widowed by police
this summer, the first artifact of a bruised life

she purged. The cat stays clear of my dogs
and me. It finds its wildness not too deeply buried.
It knows that it must capture what it can.

The Orangutans of the Omaha Zoo

The old male hid a length of wire in his lower lip
like a cut of chew, with which he'd trip the latch
of the door the keepers used to clean the grounds.
Not every day, because his life was not unhappy,

he would climb into the moat, slip the wire from his lip,
and lead his clan through the boiler room and out
into the zoo. Each time, they climbed
the tall trees by the elephant enclosure:

the old male, the fat matriarch, the juvenile
swinging his long, powerful arms, the mother
and her fuzzy-headed infant. They would wait
in those trees for the keepers to find them

tucked like nests between the narrow branches,
among the birds, the evening light, the drifting calls
of the animals behind their fences, breathing the high,
    cool air
that blew in from Wyoming and beyond.

The Fox

From the weedy margins
of the parking lot, a fox

appears, bent-headed,
and noses the line

of garbage cans. His tail,
brown and matted, thinned

at the tip, trails
along the pavement.

His fur is patched
where the last of winter's

coat remains. I still myself
along the car, as though

to quiet the entire scene.
When a screen door slams,

he raises his face,
narrow as a bird's,

into the breeze.
Along his muzzle, red

the color of embers
left burning in a fitful rain.

Centralia

These roads will take you into your own country.
   —*Muriel Rukeyser*, The Book of the Dead

I

Centralia is a town of smoke:
the houses gone, the churches boarded,
the Good Fellows Cemetery left
to the loosestrife, the goutweed, the yellow rattle;
the cracked highway and the boreholes
that emit such smoke as might drift
from a hot mouth on a winter day;
a town of remnant steps and driveways
pocked with dandelion, of vestigial stop signs,
dry hydrants, fences that the smoke ignores.

II

The fire warms the ground, which
melts the snow: in winter, Centralia
is bare and steaming, is naked
earth and browned and flattened grass.
Filaments of ice like brittle spiders
accrete along the crevices.
The vagrant fox won't hunt here,
as the voles keep to the snow.

III

If a chunk of coal kicked by a drill
cut a miner's face, he would not
bleed: coal dust stanched the flow.
These were men with spooky eyes
wide against their blackened skin
who turned the water in their showers black.
Miner's scars are blue: coal
dust in the seam. And when someone
burned his trash in an open pit
above a vein of coal, the vein
began to burn.
                        In Harrisburg, there wasn't
much to say. Let the fire snuff itself.
Nothing burns underground. (The mines
nearly gutted. A seasick drive there, anyway.)
And at first, it wasn't much: at dusk, a furry
orange glow beyond the cemetery; at noon,
a string of smoke tethering a cloud.
But then cold water started running
hot in all the houses, first at the edge
of town and then throughout. Then
someone's basement filled with poison
gas. And so the government
inspectors came
with counters and devices,
taking notes in legal
pads, calling people *neighbor*.
Dig a trench around the town, they said,
and someone did, until the funds ran out
and the trench lay half-opened like a mouth
that starts to speak and doesn't.

IV

And so Centralia burned. When a sinkhole
opened on a miner's son and pulled him in,
even the old ones said it's hell and left.
A group of men pulled the boy out
with a chain. The government
bought all the homes it could
and tore them down. And so Centralia
turned to dust. And so the fly ash
packed into the crevices swirled up like moths
when the wind rolled off the ridge. And so
the Tamaqua coal breaker shut. And so the half-
dug trench. And so the buckled road.
And so the smoke.

Forest Cemetery

I would say *clearing*
but the woods don't clear —
just a huddle of old stones
stumped like dead teeth
among the pines. Here,
where a tree has come over —
storm strike or plague beetle
or lean wind — brambles crowd
the stone. Its carved
face is long since
worn: lichen, simple
weather, perhaps once
the fingers of a mourner.
He must have lived
nearby — he and his
family must have hauled
the pine-plank coffin here
and left it in the picked hole,
what the rough ground gave
for the occasion. Then back
to the clear-cut hillside,
to the stripped log,
to the choked streams
feeding the mills. And now
this stone among a copse
of stones, hunched
on ground the forest has retaken,
this celebration of forgetting.

Notes

"On the Recording of Weldon Kees Reading 'Relating to Robinson'" describes the recording on the Poetry Foundation's website, poetryfoundation.org.

"These Fine Collapses" is for Richard Newman.

"The Cinder Woman" is based on accounts of the 1951 death by fire of Mary Hardy Reeser, considered by believers to be a case of spontaneous human combustion.

"For the Swamp King of Kalispell": The Swamp King was the name given to a huge mule deer that lived and died—of natural causes, apparently—outside Kalispell, Montana.

Since "Sonnet for the Pennsylvania Mountain Lion" was written, mountain lion sightings have been confirmed in northern Pennsylvania. Apologies to Ray.

"Dürer's Rhinoceros" owes a debt to the marvelous BBC podcast series, *A History of the World in 100 Objects.*

"The Late Deluge": The epigraphs are taken from J. M. W. Turner's own poem, "The Fallacies of Hope." The lines are among those excerpted by Turner and displayed with the paintings in 1843.

"The Orangutans of the Omaha Zoo" owes a debt to a story from WNYC's *Radiolab.*